THE RENEGADES.

DEFENDERS OF THE PLANET

FLAMES OF
AMAZONIA

DK LONDON

Editor Vicky Richards
Designer Kit Lane
Managing Editor Francesca Baines
Managing Art Editor Philip Letsu
Production Editor George Nimmo
Production Controller Sian Cheung
Jacket Designer Surabhi Wadhwa-Gandhi
Jacket Design Development Manager Sophia MTT
Publisher Andrew Mcintyre
Associate Publishing Director Liz Wheeler
Art Director Karen Self
Publishing Director Jonathan Metcalf

First published in Great Britain in 2021 by
Dorling Kindersley Limited
DK, One Embassy Gardens, 8 Viaduct Gardens,
London, SW11 7BW
The authorised representative in the EEA is Dorling Kindersley
Verlag GmbH. Arnulfstr. 124, 80636 Munich, Germany

A CIP catalogue record for this book
is available from the British Library.
ISBN: 978-0-241-4-9066-2

Printed and bound in China

For the curious
www.dk.com

This book was made with
Forest Stewardship Council™ certified paper –
one small step in DK's commitment to a sustainable future.
For more information go to www.dk.com/our-green-pledge

THE RENEGADES

DEFENDERS OF THE PLANET

VOLUME 2

CREATED BY JEREMY BROWN, KATY JAKEWAY,
ELLENOR MERERID, LIBBY REED,
AND DAVID SELBY

FLAMES OF AMAZONIA

THE AMAZON
RAINFOREST, BRAZIL

SCREEE!

MEANWHILE, IN TEXAS, USA

MORNING YOU LOT. HOW DID YOU ALL SLEEP?

ALRIGHT, THANKS --EXCEPT KATE, THAT IS.

NIGHTMARES AGAIN... I NEED TO WEAR THE ORACLE SPECS TODAY...TRY AND FIGURE IT ALL OUT.

THE DREAMS MUST MEAN *SOMETHING.* IT'S THE FOURTH TIME THIS WEEK I'VE HAD THEM.

THANKS FOR PUTTING US UP, THOUGH. THIS DEFINITELY BEATS HIDING OUT IN LONDON.

OH, PLEASE, I'M HAPPY TO! BESIDES...

...LEON'S MUM WOULD MURDER ME IF I DIDN'T LOOK AFTER HER PRECIOUS BABY BOY!

OW! FLO, I'M *LITERALLY* A SUPERHERO!

NOT ACCORDING TO THE UK GOVERNMENT, YOU'RE NOT!

WELL...

...HOW WILL THEY EVER FIND ME?

BECAUSE I KNOW YOU, LITTLE COUSIN, JUST AS I'VE GOT TO KNOW YOUR FRIENDS HERE, TOO. I KNOW YOU'RE ALREADY LOOKING FOR MORE TROUBLE!

IN OUR DEFENCE, WE DIDN'T PLAN TO HAVE TO FIGHT OFF A GIANT METHANE-BREATHING MONSTER...

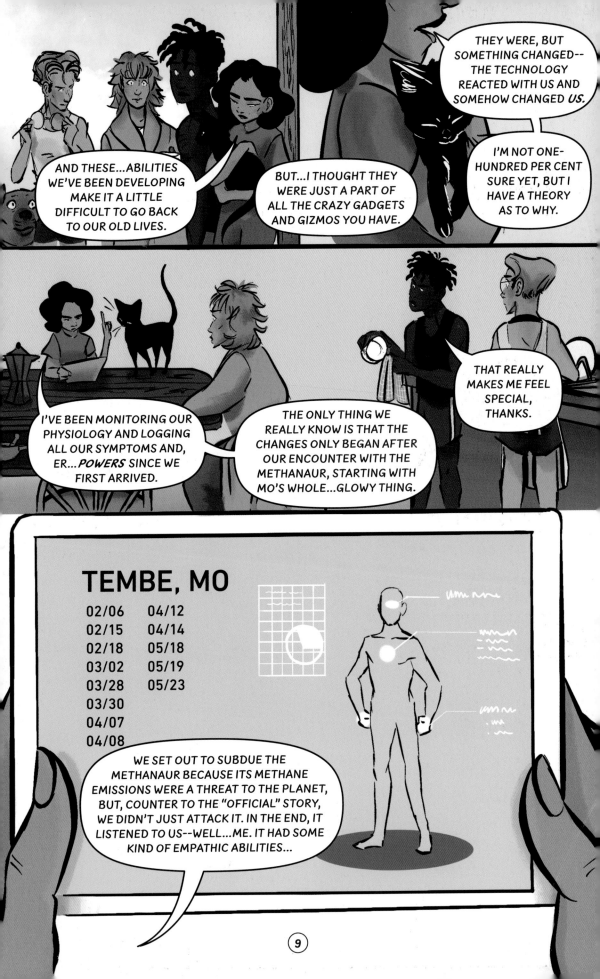

MY AI--SORRY, I FORGOT YOU NAMED HIM *STEVE*--WAS RUNNING SCANS AT THE TIME, AND HE DISCOVERED TRACES OF RADIOACTIVITY, FROM AN IMMENSE ENERGY SURGE.

DO YOU THINK THAT'S TO DO WITH MY SHIELD?

...IT'S A CREATURE UNLIKE ANYTHING I'VE MET BEFORE. I WONDER IF IT HAD MORE POWERS THAN WE REALIZED.

POSSIBLY. I THINK THE SOLAR ENERGY FROM THE SHIELD WAS CHANNELLED BY THE METHANAUR TO CAUSE OUR TECH TO *REACT WITH US*...GIVING US OUR NEW ABILITIES.

WHOA! AND IT DOESN'T SEEM TO HAVE AFFECTED YOU GUYS IN ANY PHYSICAL WAY OTHER THAN THAT...

...BUT ARE YOU ALL, Y'KNOW, *FEELING* OKAY?

RISE AND SHINE! YOU FOLKS AWAKE IN THERE?

WOW. I CAN'T BELIEVE I'M ACTUALLY HERE.

I ALWAYS DREAMED ABOUT VISITING THIS PLACE SOMEDAY.

I CAN SEE WHY--IT'S BREATHTAKING.

CLANG!

WHAT THE--?!

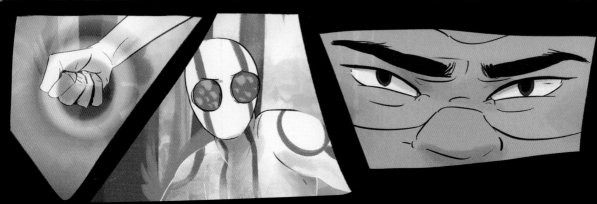

OOFT, OUCH!

STUPID STEPS, HONESTLY...

YOU'VE GOT TO BE KIDDING ME.

OKAY, I CAN EXPLAIN...

ALSO, UH, I MIGHT HAVE BROKEN SOMETHING ON YOUR PLANE, SO...MY BAD?

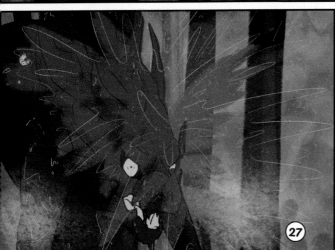

SO, UH... WHAT'S WITH THE OUTFITS?

OH, WE'RE SORT OF...A SPECIAL TEAM.

WE'RE *THE RENEGADES.*

WHY DO I FEEL LIKE WE SHOULD TAKE A BOW?

PLEASE DON'T.

OH, I'VE HEARD OF YOU! AREN'T YOU...

...VIGILANTE ECO TERRORISTS?

WE PREFER VIGILANTE *SUPERHEROES.*

DON'T BELIEVE EVERYTHING YOU READ IN THE PAPERS.

PFFT!

YOU'D NEED POWERS TO BE SUPER--

--WAIT! DO YOU HAVE POWERS?

UM, WELL, YES--

NOT HIM THOUGH, HE'S JUST TAGGING ALONG.

A GLORIFIED STOWAWAY, IF YOU WILL.

OH, GEE, THANKS.

WELL, YOU CAME HERE TO HELP, SO YOU CAN HELP ME.

I COULD USE YOU AS MY MUSCLE.

SURE! UH... HELP YOU HOW?

I'VE GOT A THEORY AS TO WHERE THESE CREATURES ARE COMING FROM, SO I WANT TO CHECK IT OUT.

ONLY ISSUE IS THAT THE PLACE I HAVE IN MIND IS HEAVILY GUARDED, SO...

JEEZ, I'M NOT CUT OUT FOR CROSS-COUNTRY!

AND YOU WERE CRITICIZING *ME* FOR NOT WORKING OUT!

SHOULD WE BE STARTING A FIRE? WHAT IF THE CREATURES SPOT US?

WE'LL TAKE THE RISK. ALTHOUGH, IN THESE PARTS, IT'S THE *JAGUARS* YOU WANT TO BE WORRIED ABOUT.

AND NO, I WON'T LET ANY OF YOU USE YOUR POWERS TO FIGHT THEM. THEY'RE ALREADY SO VULNERABLE.

WE WOULDN'T. I PROMISE! HOW LONG HAVE YOU BEEN DOING THIS?

PROTECTING THE LAND, I MEAN?

EVER SINCE I FIRST UNDERSTOOD WHAT WE WERE PROTECTING. SO...PRETTY YOUNG, YOU COULD SAY...

WE WORK TO CONSERVE THE NATIVE PLANTS AND ANIMALS, AND PROTECT THE HOMES OF THE PEOPLE WHO HAVE LIVED HERE FOR THOUSANDS OF YEARS.

...MY PEOPLE, WE DO WHAT THE GOVERNMENT WON'T.

I'VE LIVED HERE FOR MOST OF MY LIFE, EXCEPT FOR A FEW MONTHS SPENT IN THE CITY. THAT WAS...AFTER MY PARENTS WERE ARRESTED. BUT I REFUSE TO ABANDON THE FIGHT!

THE FOREST LAND ITSELF IS SACRED AND IT *DESERVES* TO BE PROTECTED. IT'S THE EARTH'S LUNGS...IT'S *BEAUTIFUL*...

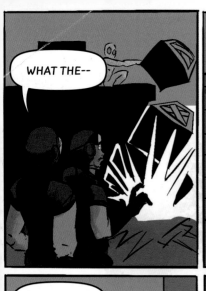

WHAT THE--

I TOLD YOU TO STRAP THOSE CRATES DOWN!

DO YOU EVER LISTEN TO ME?

RIGHT, GUARDS DISTRACTED!

ALSO, MIGHT HAVE RUINED A FRIENDSHIP, BUT IT'S ALL IN THE NAME OF SUPERHEROISM, SO HEY. PHANTOM *ONE*, POACHER NIL.

RIGHT. DO YOUR THING, SUN-BOY!

NICE WORK MO!

NOW I THINK WE SHOULD SPLIT OFF INTO GROUPS AND LOOK AROUND. I NEED TO SEE WHAT THEY'VE GOT GOING ON HERE.

MAYBE THEY HAVE A COMPUTER ROOM OR LAB--SOMETHING I CAN PRY INTO!

GREAT. SO AM I WITH SHAGGY AND SCOOBY HERE OR WITH YOU?

YOU CAN'T EVEN TELL THE DIFFERENCE BETWEEN THIS MEAT AND COW MEAT--

--BELIEVE ME, MY SCIENTISTS MADE SURE OF THAT.

THIS IS DR. MANON CARBONNEAU, MY HEAD SCIENTIST AND ONE OF THE MOST BRILLIANT MINDS I'VE EVER WORKED WITH.

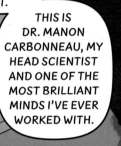

PLEASE...

IF YOU LOOK HERE, GENTLEMEN, YOU'LL SEE THAT WE'VE FABRICATED THIS CREATURE'S GENETIC CODE TO BE BARELY DISTINGUISHABLE FROM THAT OF YOUR AVERAGE COW.

SO, NOW YOU'VE GOT ALL THAT LOVELY NEW ROOM FOR CATTLE...MAY I SUGGEST THESE? AND FOR LOYAL CUSTOMERS SUCH AS YOURSELVES, I'M SURE WE CAN COME TO AN AGREEABLE PRICE.

THAT DOESN'T SOUND GOOD...

IN THE LAB

HOLY COW...THE GENETIC CODE OF THESE THINGS IS REMARKABLE.

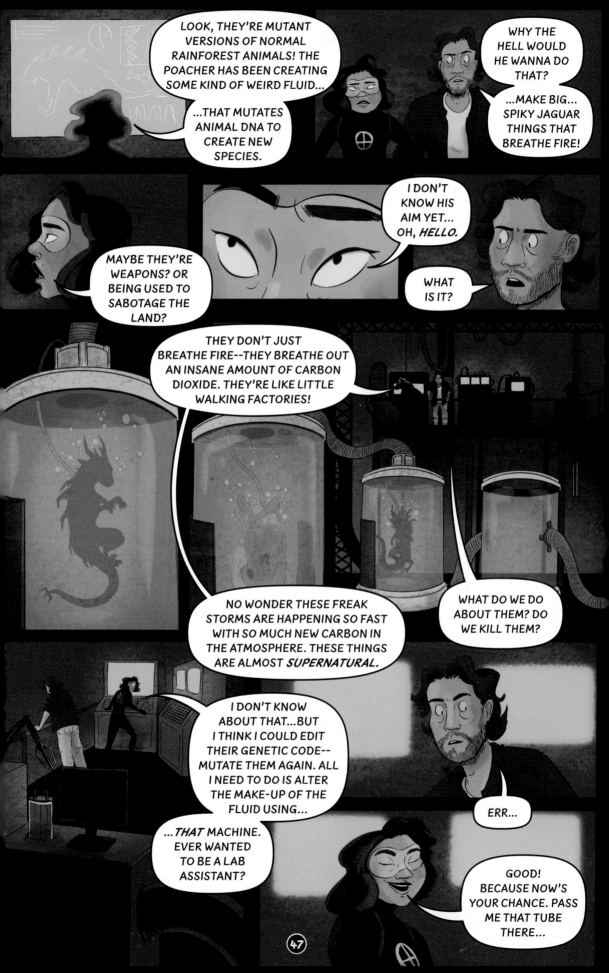

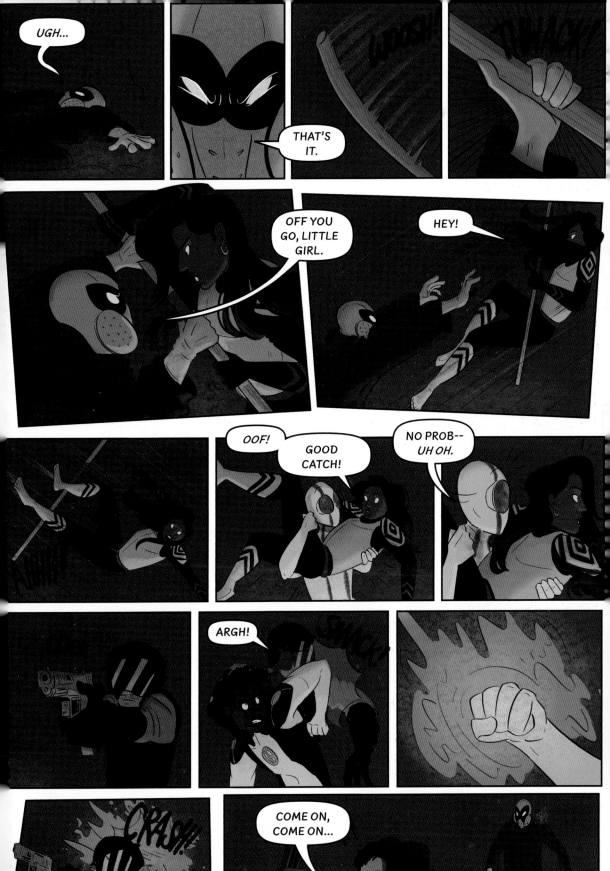

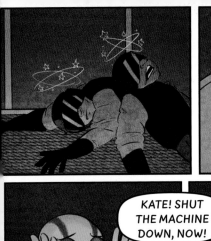

UGH...

KATE! SHUT THE MACHINE DOWN, NOW!

I AM, I AM!

OUCH!

GODDAMN KIDS.

OOF...

THAT'S GONNA NEED SOME ICE...

OH GOD...

CRACK!

SPLASH!

SLOSH

OH GOD...

IS SHE OKAY?

SHE HAS A PULSE!

WE'VE GOT TO GET HER OUT OF HERE.

WE COULD TRY AND FIND SOME MEDICAL SUPPLIES--

....?

GASP!

KATE, WHAT ARE YOU--

OH!

OH, GREAT.

JASON GREENLEAF!

HE'S THE POACHER?

CAN'T SEEM TO SHAKE YOU LOT OFF, CAN I?

I...I THINK IT ACTUALLY WORKED.

ARE YOU SURE? LIKE, COMPLETELY CERTAIN--

WHOA! AWW.

SEE? THEY'RE CALM, JUST A BIT CURIOUS.

NOT JUST FLAMEJANTE, EITHER...

WHAT ARE YOU SUPPOSED TO BE, HM?

PURRR

OOF, THAT WAS EMBARRASSING.

UH, WHAT'VE I MISSED?

OH!

ALMA! ARE YOU OKAY?!

ACTUALLY...YEAH. JUST FEELING A BIT...WEIRD--

WAIT...

WOW!

THE MACHINE... WHEN YOU FELL IN, IT MUST HAVE--

I GUESS WHATEVER YOU DID DIDN'T JUST WORK ON THE CREATURES...

HA!

WAIT!

DOES THIS MEAN I GET TO PICK OUT MY OWN SUPERHERO NAME NOW...?

SLAM!

JASON!

OH, KATELYN. IT'S BEEN SO, SO LONG.

GIVE UP. YOU'RE SURROUNDED.

AHH, BUT NOT YET DEFEATED. SEE, THIS BUTTON WILL RELEASE ALL THE CREATURES FROM THIS CONTAINER PARK, INCLUDING THE FLAMEJANTE.

THEY'LL HEAD STRAIGHT TO THE FACTORY, AND BURN IT AND THE FOREST TO THE GROUND.

IF YOU PRESS IT, I'LL KILL YOU!

HA HA HA

YOUR LITTLE ELECTRIC GLOVE DOESN'T SCARE ME. PLUS, IT'S TOO LATE. I'VE ALREADY PRESSED IT.

OH NO...

DEAD MAN'S SWITCH, OF A KIND. THE SECOND I LIFT MY FINGER OFF THE BUTTON, THE CREATURES ARE RELEASED.

WHICH MEANS... KILLING ME IS THE LAST THING ANY OF YOU WANT TO DO.

SO...KATELYN, WHY DON'T YOU INTRODUCE ME TO YOUR FRIENDS?

FINE... THIS IS M--

NO!

BEEP!

GROOOOOWL!

CONTAINER DOORS OPENING!

HISSsss...

GRRR

RAAHH!

GRUUGH!

BRR!

BEEP!

SCREEEEEEE!

UGH!

HMM, THAT DID STING A BIT.

W-WHAT?

THAT, MY FRIEND, IS WHAT WE CALL "LEVELLING THE PLAYING FIELD."

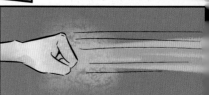

NOW, YOU ALL HAVE TWO OPTIONS. YOU CAN STAY HERE AND FIGHT ME, FAIR AND SQUARE, OR YOU CAN GO BACK TO THE FACTORY AND SAVE YOUR FRIENDS. BUT YOU CAN'T DO BOTH.

YOU MIGHT BE ABLE TO BEAT ME, BUT IT WILL BE AT THE COST OF YOUR FRIENDS' *LIVES.* AND YOU MIGHT BE ABLE TO SAVE YOUR FRIENDS, BUT IT WILL BE AT THE COST OF MY ESCAPE.

WHAT'S IT TO BE?

GO.

KATE--

WHAT?!

GO. I'LL BE RIGHT BEHIND YOU.

C'MON, WE'VE GOT TO...

...LOOK AT US NOW.

ALL THOSE YEARS WORKING TOGETHER...

MEANWHILE, OUTSIDE THE FACTORY

I DOUBLE-CHECKED THE BUILDING. I THINK EVERYONE'S OUT--

BEEP!

BEEP!

WHAT THE DAMN HECK IS GOING ON?!

ALERT! FACILITY BREACH!

BEEP!

D'YA THINK IT'S THE POACHER?

COULD BE--

YOU CAME BACK!

WE DIDN'T STOP GREENLEAF IN TIME. HE'S RELEASED THE CREATURES FROM THE CONTAINER PARK, AND THEY'RE HEADING THIS WAY.

COULDN'T LEAVE OUR FAVOURITE ACTIVIST ON HER OWN, COULD WE?

YOU'RE GONNA NEED OUR HELP.

IF THEY DESTROY THE FACTORY, WE WON'T HAVE ANY PROOF OF JASON'S WORK.

IF WE CAN'T SAVE THE PLANET, THEN WE HAVE TO SAVE OURSELVES...

MAKE OUR BODIES BETTER AND STRONGER--

--IMMUNE TO HEAT, FIRE, FLOODING, AND PREDATORS. *YOU'VE* CHANGED, AND SO HAVE I, BUT WE COULD TRANSFORM THE ENTIRE *WORLD.*

BUT-- NO! YOU WOULDN'T!

THAT WOULD INVOLVE MAKING EVERYONE YOUR EQUALS.

AND THAT'S ONE THING YOU'D NEVER DO.

I'D HAVE THE FAME, THE GLORY...

...AND I WOULDN'T HAVE TO MAKE THE "SACRIFICES" YOU KEEP DEMANDING.

WE WOULDN'T HAVE TO WORRY ABOUT FACTORY EMISSIONS, AND PRIVATE JETS, AND PLASTICS IN THE OCEAN. WE'D SURVIVE IT ALL!

AND THE NATURAL WORLD? YOU'D JUST LEAVE THE ANIMAL KINGDOM TO DIE.

YOU'D LET ALL OF THIS PLANET BURN?!

PERHAPS. OR THE ANIMAL KINGDOM COULD ASCEND WITH US AS A BETTER, STRONGER FORM OF LIFE.

A *PERMANENT* SOLUTION. WHAT DO YOU THINK?

SLAM!

CENTRO DE CONTROLE

I, UM--

LEON!

I CAME BACK TO...ER...

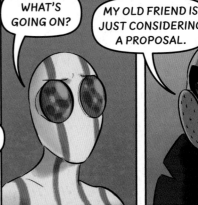

WHAT'S GOING ON?

MY OLD FRIEND IS JUST CONSIDERING A PROPOSAL.

KATE?

JUST THINK, IF YOU WORKED WITH ME, YOU COULD HAVE A SHARE OF THAT GLORY.

LOOK AT YOU NOW-- HIDING FROM THE WORLD, FROM YOURSELF, ALONE EVERY NIGHT WITH YOUR GUILT...

...ALL BECAUSE YOU THINK HELPING ME FOR ALL THOSE YEARS WAS EVIL. BUT YOU COULD PROVE THAT WE WERE *RIGHT* THE WHOLE TIME.

WHAT'S HAPPENING?

SHE MOVED ON! FROM...ALL THIS, FROM YOU!

OH...

I DON'T THINK SHE *EVER* DID THAT.

WE DID WHAT WE COULD, FOLKS...

...BUT WE COULDN'T SAVE IT ALL.

THE RAINFOREST BURNS EVERY DAY. WHEN YOU THINK ABOUT THE BIGGER PICTURE, THIS IS NOTHING IN COMPARISON.

BUT STILL...

ALMA, ARE YOU OKAY?

YEAH... YEAH, I'M ALRIGHT.

COME ON--

--LET'S GO GET OUR FRIENDS.

I KNOW EXACTLY WHERE I STAND, AND I SEE YOU FOR *EXACTLY* WHO YOU ARE.

YOU'VE NOT CHANGED--THIS IS STILL *BUSINESS* TO YOU! YOU HAVE NO DESIRE TO HELP HUMANITY. NO, YOU JUST WANT TO BETTER YOURSELF.

OH, PLEASE--

IT'S ALL JUST A BUSINESS PLAN! SIMPLE AS.

FACILITATE BUSINESSES THAT SPEED UP THE PLANET'S DESTRUCTION, THEN EVERYONE WILL HAVE TO COME CRAWLING BACK TO YOU.

OH, I SEE...AND THEN EVERYONE HAS TO *BUY* YOUR SERUM TO SURVIVE.

IT'S INEVITABLE.

THE PLANET IS ALREADY CHANGING. BUT WE DON'T NEED TO CHANGE IT--

--WE JUST NEED TO CHANGE OURSELVES.

THE CLIMATE EMERGENCY

WHILE FIRE-BREATHING CREATURES LIKE FLAMEJANTE MIGHT BE A WORK OF FICTION, THE THREAT OF CLIMATE CHANGE IS VERY REAL AND AFFECTS US ALL. TO HAVE ANY CHANCE OF PREVENTING THE PLANET FROM WARMING FURTHER WE NEED TO ACT NOW, SO IT'S IMPORTANT TO UNDERSTAND THE SCIENCE OF CLIMATE CHANGE--THE CAUSES, THE EFFECTS, AND WHAT WE CAN DO ABOUT IT.

WHAT IS CLIMATE CHANGE?

The Earth is warmed by a layer of gases in the atmosphere that trap heat from the Sun. But many human activities release gases that contribute to this effect, such as carbon dioxide. These gases build up in the atmosphere trapping more heat, like the glass of a greenhouse, and causing the climate of our planet to warm much faster than usual. This effect is called global warming and has many impacts on Earth's climate, causing sea levels to rise and more extreme weather events to occur.

WHY ARE EARTH'S FORESTS IMPORTANT?

Forests are known as "carbon sinks" because of trees' ability to absorb carbon dioxide from the air. When forests are burned down, not only are carbon sinks lost, but carbon dioxide is released into the atmosphere, adding to the greenhouse effect. Forests, and rainforests especially, are also home to a large proportion of the world's animal and plant species.

DEFORESTATION AND FARMING

Deforestation has increased in recent years, with land being cleared to graze cattle and grow animal feed, and for crops such as soy and palm oil. In Brazil, the actions of big companies and pressures on farmers have caused large parts of the Amazon rainforest to be burnt to make way for agriculture. In July 2019, an area the size of five football pitches was cleared there every minute.

WHAT ARE THE CONSEQUENCES?

Deforestation is having a major impact on our planet. As well as adding to the build-up of greenhouse gases, accelerating the effects of climate change, it is destroying habitats – putting the biodiversity of animal and plant species under threat. Deforestation also forces animals into closer contact with humans, and increases the risk of them passing on diseases.

DEFENDING THE FOREST

More than 80 per cent of the Earth's biodiversity is protected by indigenous people. Many of these communities have a spiritual relationship with the Earth that has fuelled their activism against land theft and destruction. But the work of eco-activists can put them into conflict with powerful groups. Influential Lenca and Honduran campaigner Berta Cáceres was assassinated in 2016, and many other activists have been killed.

SUCCESS STORIES

It is possible to prevent deforestation, by paying farmers to protect the trees, and developing eco-tourism and more eco-friendly types of agriculture and forestry. In one such project in Costa Rica, species like sloths and tree frogs can now live amongst crops like organic pineapple!

WHAT CAN WE DO?

Learning from case studies and the knowledge and practices of many local groups, everyone has the power to urge governments to pass laws to defend the forests, and to push big businesses to farm in a way that respects human rights, and the soil and water we depend on.

MEET THE TEAM

THE RENEGADES COMICS ARE CREATED BY A PASSIONATE TEAM, BROUGHT TOGETHER BY THEIR DRIVE TO PROTECT THE CLIMATE.

HOW TO HELP THE PLANET

As well as pushing for governments to act, there are lots of things we can do to help the planet, such as eating less meat and other foods linked to climate change. Did you know plant-based foods cause less greenhouse gas emissions than many meats? To explore more about topics like these, visit our website down below!

JEREMY BROWN *THE RENEGADES* WAS CO-FOUNDED BY JEREMY WHILE HE STUDIED FOR A MASTERS IN CLIMATE CHANGE AT KING'S COLLEGE LONDON. ALONGSIDE DREAMING UP THE CHARACTERS AND STORY ARCS, HE ENJOYS A SPOT OF POLITICS AND STAND-UP COMEDY.

KATY JAKEWAY WHILE CREATING *THE RENEGADES*, KATY WAS ALSO STUDYING AT KING'S COLLEGE LONDON. KATY JOINED THE PROJECT IN ITS EARLY DAYS, USING HER PASSION FOR ART AND WRITING TO HELP BRING JEREMY'S INITIAL IDEAS TO LIFE.

DAVID SELBY CO-SCRIPTWRITER OF *THE RENEGADES* AND FELLOW FORMER KING'S COLLEGE LONDON STUDENT, DAVID WAS KEEN TO BUILD ON JEREMY AND KATY'S IDEAS, AND HOPES TO SEE THE PROJECT RAISE AWARENESS ABOUT CLIMATE CHANGE.

KATY JAKEWAY

ELLENOR MERERID

JEREMY BROWN

LIBBY REED

DAVID SELBY

LIBBY REED LIBBY SPENDS MOST OF HER TIME DRAWING AND MAKING UP STORIES. SHE LOVES ANIMALS, ESPECIALLY REPTILES, AND USES HER ARTWORK TO SHOW THE BEAUTY OF THE NATURAL WORLD.

ELLENOR MERERID ELLENOR IS INSPIRED BY DAVID ATTENBOROUGH AND CHARLES DARWIN — PEOPLE WHO HAVE SHOWN THE MIGHT AND MIRACLE OF OUR PLANET TO MILLIONS OF PEOPLE. ELLENOR LIKES FOLKLORE AND STARGAZING.

ACKNOWLEDGEMENTS SPECIAL THANKS TO SUFFOLK FRIEND AND COMIC GEEK MISCHA PEARSON FOR PIONEERING THE GUARDIANS OF THE PLANET (THE PREDECESSOR TO THE RENEGADES). MUCH CREDIT TO COURSEMATES JONATHAN HYDE, TOM HAMBLEY, AND ELIAS YASSIN FOR THEIR GEOGRAPHICAL WISDOM, BOLD ACTIVISM, AND LOYAL FRIENDSHIP, WHICH ALL VERY MUCH HELPED TO SHAPE THE COMIC. THERE ARE TOO MANY TO LIST HERE, BUT A BIG THANK YOU ALSO TO JAMES PORTER, KATE SCHRECKENBERG, GEORGE ADAMSON, ODHRAN LINSEY, MICHAEL BARNARD, PARAS SINGH AND ALL THE LOVELY CREW AT DK FOR THEIR ENTHUSIASM, PATIENCE, AND COMMITMENT TO PROTECTING THE PLANET THROUGH STORYTELLING. DK WOULD LIKE TO THANK HAZEL BEYNON FOR PROOFREADING.

CHECK OUT OUR WEBSITE **RENEGADESCOMIC.ORG** FOR THE LATEST TIPS ON WHAT YOU CAN DO TO DEFEND THE PLANET YOURSELF!